PRINCEWILL LAGANG

Intrapreneurship: Igniting Innovation from Within

First published by PRINCEWILL LAGANG 2023

Copyright © 2023 by Princewill Lagang

All rights reserved. No part of this publication may be reproduced, stored or transmitted in any form or by any means, electronic, mechanical, photocopying, recording, scanning, or otherwise without written permission from the publisher. It is illegal to copy this book, post it to a website, or distribute it by any other means without permission.

Princewill Lagang asserts the moral right to be identified as the author of this work.

First edition

This book was professionally typeset on Reedsy.
Find out more at reedsy.com

Contents

1	Intrapreneurship: Igniting Innovation from Within	1
2	The Anatomy of an Intrapreneur	4
3	Fostering Intrapreneurship: Strategies and Tools	7
4	Overcoming Challenges in Intrapreneurship	11
5	Scaling Intrapreneurship for Organizational Impact	15
6	The Future of Intrapreneurship	19
7	Nurturing Your Inner Intrapreneur	23
8	Sustaining Intrapreneurship for Long-Term Success	27
9	Overcoming Common Pitfalls in Intrapreneurship	31
10	Intrapreneurship in the 21st Century	35
11	The Future of Intrapreneurship	39
12	Fostering Intrapreneurship Culture	44

1

Intrapreneurship: Igniting Innovation from Within

The sun hung low in the sky, casting a warm, golden hue over the sleek, modern office building that stood as a testament to human ingenuity and enterprise. Inside, the hum of productivity filled the air as employees bustled about their daily tasks, while the promise of innovation permeated every corner of the space. This was the headquarters of GlobalTech Innovations, a dynamic and forward-thinking technology company that had risen to prominence through a commitment to intrapreneurship.

Intrapreneurship is a term that you may have heard before, or perhaps it's entirely new to you. In this first chapter, we will dive deep into the concept of intrapreneurship, exploring its definition, origins, and the critical role it plays in fostering innovation within organizations. As we embark on this journey, we will meet several individuals whose experiences and stories will serve as windows into the world of intrapreneurship, showing how it can transform businesses and individuals alike.

Defining Intrapreneurship

To grasp the essence of intrapreneurship, we must start with its definition. At its core, intrapreneurship is the practice of cultivating an entrepreneurial mindset and spirit within an existing organization, allowing employees to act as "intrapreneurs" by pursuing new, innovative projects or initiatives. Intrapreneurs are the visionaries within a company, individuals who identify opportunities for growth and progress, and are empowered to bring their ideas to life within the corporate structure. This can encompass developing new products or services, improving existing processes, or exploring uncharted markets. Intrapreneurs are the innovators who spark change from within, much like the pioneers of the tech industry who disrupt the status quo with groundbreaking products and services.

Origins of Intrapreneurship

The concept of intrapreneurship finds its roots in the work of Howard Stevenson, a professor at Harvard Business School, who coined the term "intrapreneur" in the late 1970s. Stevenson envisioned intrapreneurs as employees who demonstrate the same qualities and behaviors as entrepreneurs, despite working within the confines of a larger organization. His groundbreaking insights laid the foundation for the understanding and cultivation of intrapreneurship, which has since gained widespread recognition as a powerful driver of corporate innovation.

The Importance of Intrapreneurship

Why is intrapreneurship so important in today's rapidly evolving business landscape? The answer lies in the ever-increasing pace of change, competition, and technological advancements. In a world where the only constant is change, organizations that do not innovate risk obsolescence. Intrapreneurship acts as the antidote to stagnation, allowing companies to adapt, grow, and thrive. It nurtures a culture of innovation that inspires employees to embrace new challenges, explore uncharted territory, and take calculated risks, all while staying tethered to the organization's mission and values.

As we explore intrapreneurship further, you'll learn how companies like GlobalTech Innovations have harnessed the power of intrapreneurship to remain at the forefront of their industries. You'll also discover the skills and attributes that make a successful intrapreneur and the tools and strategies that organizations employ to encourage and support intrapreneurial initiatives.

But first, let us meet Sarah, a determined and imaginative intrapreneur at GlobalTech Innovations, whose journey from idea to innovation will illustrate the concept of intrapreneurship in action. Through her story, you will gain insight into the challenges and triumphs that intrapreneurs face as they strive to ignite innovation from within the corporate world.

2

The Anatomy of an Intrapreneur

Intrapreneurs are the lifeblood of innovation within organizations, embodying the spirit of entrepreneurship while operating within the corporate framework. In this chapter, we will delve into the qualities, characteristics, and skills that define successful intrapreneurs. To do this, we will closely examine the journey of Sarah, the intrapreneur we met in the previous chapter, as she navigates the complex landscape of corporate innovation at GlobalTech Innovations.

The Birth of an Intrapreneur

Sarah was not always an intrapreneur. Like many of us, she started her career as an enthusiastic and driven employee, excelling in her assigned tasks but feeling the itch for something more. Her journey towards becoming an intrapreneur began when she noticed a gap in the market, an opportunity that her organization had yet to exploit.

Vision and Innovation

One of the hallmark traits of an intrapreneur is a clear and compelling vision. Sarah saw potential where others saw challenges. She envisioned a new product that could revolutionize how people interact with technology, and she couldn't shake the feeling that she needed to bring this vision to life. Intrapreneurs possess the ability to see possibilities where others see limitations, and they have a passion for turning these possibilities into reality.

Courage and Risk-Taking

Intrapreneurs are not risk-averse. Sarah knew that championing her idea was a gamble, but she was willing to take the risk. Intrapreneurs are unafraid of challenging the status quo and pushing boundaries. They embrace calculated risks and are ready to face potential setbacks head-on. This courage often sets them apart from the traditional corporate employee.

Resilience

As Sarah's journey unfolded, she encountered numerous roadblocks and obstacles. Her project faced skepticism, budget constraints, and internal politics. Yet, intrapreneurs possess a tenacious spirit. They do not back down easily when confronted with adversity. Sarah learned to adapt, pivot, and persevere, which is a key trait of successful intrapreneurs.

Innovative Problem-Solving

Intrapreneurs excel in innovative problem-solving. They approach challenges with a creative mindset and a knack for finding solutions where others might see dead ends. Sarah had to think outside the box to secure the resources and support needed for her project. Intrapreneurs bring a unique problem-solving perspective that can catalyze transformation within an organization.

Networking and Collaboration

Successful intrapreneurs understand the value of collaboration. Sarah actively sought out mentors, allies, and champions within the organization who shared her vision. She also engaged with experts from various departments to gain insights and support for her project. Intrapreneurs possess strong interpersonal skills, fostering relationships that are crucial to their success.

Strategic Thinking

Intrapreneurs are strategic thinkers. Sarah created a well-thought-out plan for her project, aligning it with GlobalTech Innovations' overarching goals and strategies. She recognized that her intrapreneurial efforts had to complement the organization's mission and values. This ability to connect the dots and integrate intrapreneurial initiatives into the corporate strategy is a hallmark of effective intrapreneurs.

Measuring Impact

Intrapreneurs are results-oriented. Sarah continuously monitored and evaluated the impact of her project, making data-driven decisions and adapting her strategy as needed. Successful intrapreneurs understand the importance of measuring and communicating the value they bring to the organization.

Sarah's journey from a motivated employee to a successful intrapreneur exemplifies the qualities and attributes that define intrapreneurs. As we continue this chapter, we will explore how GlobalTech Innovations recognized and supported these characteristics in Sarah, and how other organizations can cultivate intrapreneurial talent within their ranks. The next chapter will provide a closer look at the strategies and tools that organizations use to foster intrapreneurship and ignite innovation from within.

3

Fostering Intrapreneurship: Strategies and Tools

In the previous chapter, we explored the qualities and attributes of intrapreneurs through the journey of Sarah, an intrapreneur at GlobalTech Innovations. In this chapter, we will delve into the strategies and tools that organizations can use to cultivate and support intrapreneurship within their ranks. Just as intrapreneurs play a vital role in sparking innovation, organizations must create an environment that encourages and empowers these entrepreneurial thinkers.

Cultivating a Culture of Intrapreneurship

Intrapreneurship thrives in an environment that fosters innovation, encourages risk-taking, and values employee contributions. Creating a culture of intrapreneurship is foundational to the success of intrapreneurs like Sarah.

1. Leadership Support: Leadership must be committed to fostering intrapreneurship. They should not only endorse but actively participate in initiatives that encourage employees to innovate. This sends a clear message

that intrapreneurship is not only allowed but celebrated.

2. Autonomy and Empowerment: Intrapreneurs need the freedom to experiment and make decisions. They should be empowered to take ownership of their projects and have the autonomy to see them through. GlobalTech Innovations, for example, provides intrapreneurs like Sarah with the resources and support needed to pursue their vision.

3. Resource Allocation: Organizations must allocate resources, including time and budget, for intrapreneurial initiatives. Whether it's through dedicated innovation funds or designated work hours, resource allocation is essential for intrapreneurs to realize their ideas.

4. Risk Tolerance: A culture of intrapreneurship should include an acceptance of failure as part of the innovation process. Encouraging calculated risks and learning from failures is crucial to intrapreneurial success.

Intrapreneurial Support Programs

To empower intrapreneurs, organizations can establish specific programs and tools:

1. Intrapreneurial Incubators: These are structured environments that provide support, mentorship, and resources to intrapreneurs as they develop their projects. Incubators can facilitate collaboration and networking among intrapreneurs.

2. Innovation Challenges: Organizations can periodically host innovation challenges that invite employees to submit their ideas. Winning proposals can receive funding and support for development.

3. Intrapreneurial Training: Offer training programs that help employees develop the skills and mindset required for intrapreneurship. This can include

courses on creative thinking, problem-solving, and project management.

4. Recognition and Rewards: Acknowledging and rewarding intrapreneurial efforts is essential. Recognition can come in various forms, such as bonuses, promotions, or public acknowledgment of successful projects.

Innovation Management Platforms

To facilitate intrapreneurial projects, organizations can invest in digital innovation management platforms that help streamline the process:

1. Idea Submission: These platforms allow employees to submit and share their ideas, creating a centralized repository for innovation within the company.

2. Project Tracking: Organizations can use project management tools to monitor the progress of intrapreneurial initiatives, making it easier to allocate resources and measure impact.

3. Collaboration Tools: Implementing collaboration software can help intrapreneurs and their teams work together seamlessly, even if they are in different locations.

4. Data Analytics: Incorporating data analytics into the platform allows organizations to measure the success of intrapreneurial projects and make data-driven decisions.

Measuring Intrapreneurial Success

To assess the impact of intrapreneurship on the organization, it's essential to have key performance indicators (KPIs) in place. These may include:

1. Innovation Metrics: These metrics can measure the number of successful

intrapreneurial projects, their impact on revenue, and their alignment with the organization's strategic goals.

2. Employee Engagement: Assessing the level of employee engagement in intrapreneurial activities is crucial. High engagement can be a sign of a healthy intrapreneurship culture.

3. Financial Performance: Evaluate the return on investment (ROI) of intrapreneurial initiatives, looking at revenue generated, cost savings, or market share gained.

In this chapter, we've explored the strategies and tools that organizations can use to encourage and support intrapreneurship. As we move forward, we will continue to learn from Sarah's journey and the experiences of other intrapreneurs to gain a deeper understanding of how organizations can unlock the innovative potential within their employees.

4

Overcoming Challenges in Intrapreneurship

Intrapreneurship is not without its hurdles and obstacles. Just as with any innovation-driven endeavor, intrapreneurs often face challenges that can test their resolve and creativity. In this chapter, we'll explore some of the common challenges intrapreneurs encounter and how they can navigate these difficulties effectively. To do this, we'll draw from Sarah's experiences at GlobalTech Innovations and her journey as an intrapreneur.

Internal Resistance and Skepticism

One of the primary challenges intrapreneurs like Sarah face is internal resistance. Many colleagues or even superiors may be skeptical about new ideas or reluctant to change established processes. It's essential for intrapreneurs to address this resistance by:

- Building a Convincing Case: Intrapreneurs must be adept at presenting a compelling business case that demonstrates the potential benefits of their idea. Sarah, for example, used market research and financial projections to back her proposal.

- Seeking Allies: Identifying and enlisting the support of allies within the organization is crucial. These allies can help champion the intrapreneurial project and influence key stakeholders.

Resource Constraints

Limited resources, whether in terms of funding, time, or personnel, can be a significant roadblock for intrapreneurs. To overcome this challenge, intrapreneurs should:

- Optimize Resource Allocation: Carefully manage and allocate available resources. This includes exploring cost-effective solutions, leveraging existing infrastructure, and seeking alternative funding sources.

- Advocate for Investment: Make a persuasive case for the necessary resources, highlighting the potential return on investment and the strategic importance of the project.

Corporate Bureaucracy

In large organizations, navigating the bureaucracy and complex decision-making processes can be daunting. Intrapreneurs can address this challenge by:

- Leveraging Supportive Leadership: Engage with leaders who support intrapreneurial initiatives and can help navigate the corporate hierarchy.

- Streamlining Processes: If possible, work on streamlining and expediting approval and decision-making processes to avoid unnecessary delays.

Balancing Intrapreneurial Freedom with Organizational Alignment

Finding the right balance between intrapreneurial freedom and alignment with the organization's goals can be a delicate challenge. Intrapreneurs should:

- Regularly Communicate: Maintain open communication with organizational leadership to ensure that intrapreneurial initiatives remain aligned with strategic objectives.

- Periodic Evaluation: Continuously assess the alignment of intrapreneurial projects with the organization's mission and make adjustments as necessary.

Dealing with Failure

Not all intrapreneurial projects succeed. Failure is an inherent part of innovation, and intrapreneurs must cope with disappointments. To manage this challenge, intrapreneurs can:

- Learn and Pivot: Treat failures as learning opportunities. Identify what went wrong, adjust strategies, and use the experience to improve future initiatives.

- Maintain Resilience: Develop resilience and a growth mindset. Recognize that setbacks are part of the innovation journey and are not personal failures.

Sustainability and Scalability

Scaling a successful intrapreneurial project can present its own set of challenges. Intrapreneurs should:

- Develop Scalability Plans: Consider scalability from the project's inception, preparing for growth while maintaining quality and efficiency.

- Ensure Sustainability: Assess the long-term sustainability of the project, including its impact on the organization and the market.

Ethical and Social Responsibility Considerations

Intrapreneurs must also consider the ethical and social responsibility implications of their projects. This can involve addressing questions related to environmental impact, labor practices, and community engagement.

- Ethical Guidelines: Organizations should provide guidelines and ethical considerations that intrapreneurs must adhere to when developing their projects.

- Stakeholder Engagement: Engage with stakeholders, including employees, customers, and the community, to ensure that the project's impact is positive and aligned with corporate values.

In this chapter, we've explored the challenges intrapreneurs may face and the strategies they can employ to overcome them. Through Sarah's experiences at GlobalTech Innovations and the experiences of other intrapreneurs, we've seen that with determination, resilience, and the right approaches, intrapreneurs can navigate these challenges and drive meaningful innovation within their organizations.

5

Scaling Intrapreneurship for Organizational Impact

Intrapreneurship, when nurtured and managed effectively, has the potential to drive significant organizational impact. In this chapter, we'll explore how organizations can scale their intrapreneurship initiatives to maximize innovation, create a sustainable intrapreneurial ecosystem, and achieve broader strategic goals. We will continue to draw insights from Sarah's experiences at GlobalTech Innovations and examine best practices from other successful intrapreneurial programs.

Building an Intrapreneurial Ecosystem

To scale intrapreneurship within an organization, it's essential to create an ecosystem that supports and sustains intrapreneurial activities. This ecosystem involves the following key elements:

1. Leadership Commitment: Top-level leadership must not only endorse but actively champion intrapreneurship. Their commitment sets the tone for the entire organization and signals the importance of innovation.

2. Clear Vision and Strategy: Develop a clear intrapreneurship vision and strategy aligned with the organization's broader mission and goals. Ensure that intrapreneurship is integrated into the organizational culture and values.

3. Resource Allocation: Allocate dedicated resources for intrapreneurial projects. This may involve setting aside budgets, providing access to facilities, and offering time for employees to work on their initiatives.

4. Incubators and Innovation Hubs: Establish physical or virtual spaces where intrapreneurs can collaborate, experiment, and develop their ideas. These spaces should facilitate creativity and networking.

5. Intrapreneurial Training: Offer ongoing training programs to help employees develop intrapreneurial skills, such as problem-solving, risk management, and creative thinking.

6. Feedback Loops: Implement feedback mechanisms that allow intrapreneurs to receive input and insights from colleagues, mentors, and leadership. This feedback loop fosters learning and improvement.

Collaboration and Cross-Functional Teams

Intrapreneurship thrives on collaboration. To scale intrapreneurship, organizations should promote cross-functional teams and interdepartmental collaboration. This approach:

- Encourages diversity of thought and expertise.
    - Fosters innovative solutions that draw from multiple disciplines.
    - Enhances the chances of project success by tapping into a broader pool of resources and knowledge.

Internal and External Networking

Establishing and maintaining a network of intrapreneurs, mentors, advisors, and experts is crucial. Encourage intrapreneurs to connect both within and outside the organization. Benefits include:

- Sharing best practices and learning from others.
    - Gaining external perspectives and insights.
    - Building relationships that can lead to partnerships, investments, and market opportunities.

Scalable Innovation Management Platforms

Invest in innovation management platforms that can scale as the number of intrapreneurial projects grows. These platforms should include:

- Idea Generation and Submission: A centralized system for collecting and evaluating intrapreneurial proposals.
    - Project Tracking and Management: Tools for monitoring the progress and impact of intrapreneurial initiatives.
    - Collaboration and Communication: Software that fosters teamwork and communication across diverse teams.
    - Data Analytics: Systems to measure and evaluate the success of intrapreneurial projects.

Continuous Learning and Adaptation

Intrapreneurship is an evolving field, and organizations should continuously learn and adapt to stay relevant. Encourage a culture of experimentation and the willingness to pivot when needed. Learning from both successes and failures is critical for long-term sustainability.

Recognition and Rewards

Recognize and reward successful intrapreneurs to incentivize further innovation. These rewards can take various forms, such as financial incentives, promotions, and public recognition. Acknowledging intrapreneurs' contributions reinforces the organization's commitment to intrapreneurship.

Measuring Impact and Accountability

To ensure that intrapreneurship is contributing to the organization's strategic objectives, establish clear key performance indicators (KPIs) and accountability mechanisms. Regularly assess the impact of intrapreneurial initiatives on revenue, cost savings, and other relevant metrics.

In this chapter, we've explored the strategies and practices for scaling intrapreneurship within organizations, drawing from the experiences of intrapreneurs like Sarah and successful intrapreneurial programs. As organizations cultivate a culture of intrapreneurship and create a supportive ecosystem, they can harness the full potential of intrapreneurial innovation and achieve lasting impact.

6

The Future of Intrapreneurship

Intrapreneurship has already made significant strides in transforming the way organizations innovate and adapt to the ever-evolving business landscape. However, the future promises even more exciting developments and opportunities for intrapreneurship. In this chapter, we will explore the emerging trends, challenges, and potential pathways that will shape the future of intrapreneurship.

Technological Advancements

In an age of rapid technological progress, intrapreneurship will continue to be closely intertwined with innovation. The following technological advancements will significantly impact intrapreneurship in the future:

- Artificial Intelligence and Machine Learning: These technologies will be increasingly utilized to analyze market trends, customer behavior, and project viability, providing intrapreneurs with valuable insights for their initiatives.

- Blockchain and Decentralized Finance (DeFi): These innovations will offer new opportunities for intrapreneurs, especially in the realm of finance and supply chain management.

- Virtual Reality (VR) and Augmented Reality (AR): These technologies will enhance product development, design, and customer engagement, creating fertile ground for intrapreneurial initiatives.

- Advanced Data Analytics: As data becomes more abundant, intrapreneurs will have access to powerful analytics tools that can help them make data-driven decisions and refine their projects.

Global Collaboration and Remote Work

The rise of remote work and global collaboration will expand the pool of potential intrapreneurs. As teams become more diverse and geographically dispersed, organizations will need to adapt their intrapreneurship programs to facilitate and harness this global talent.

- Digital Collaboration Tools: The development of more advanced collaboration and project management tools will enable intrapreneurs to work effectively across borders.

- Cultural Sensitivity: Understanding and respecting diverse cultural norms and expectations will become essential for successful intrapreneurship in a global context.

Environmental and Social Responsibility

The future of intrapreneurship will see an increasing focus on projects that contribute to sustainability and social responsibility. Organizations will encourage intrapreneurs to develop solutions that address environmental concerns, ethical business practices, and community well-being.

- Sustainability Initiatives: Intrapreneurs will be empowered to create products and processes that reduce the environmental footprint of their organizations.

- Social Impact Projects: Intrapreneurs will work on initiatives that benefit the community and underprivileged populations, reflecting a growing trend towards social entrepreneurship.

Evolving Organizational Structures

The hierarchy of traditional corporate structures is gradually giving way to flatter, more flexible organizations that are better suited to intrapreneurship. These changes will shape the future of how intrapreneurs operate:

- Matrix Organizations: Intrapreneurs will navigate complex, matrix-style organizations, collaborating with diverse teams and reporting to multiple managers.

- Holacracy and Self-Management: Some organizations may adopt self-management systems like holacracy, giving intrapreneurs greater autonomy and decision-making authority.

Regulatory Challenges and Ethical Considerations

As intrapreneurship expands, it will encounter a range of regulatory challenges and ethical dilemmas. The future of intrapreneurship will require organizations and intrapreneurs to navigate these complexities, such as data privacy, intellectual property rights, and ethical decision-making.

- Compliance and Regulation: Organizations will need to stay vigilant about compliance with evolving regulations related to innovation and data security.

- Ethical Guidelines: Organizations will establish clear ethical guidelines to guide intrapreneurs in making responsible decisions.

Adaptive Learning and Development Programs

In the future, learning and development programs for intrapreneurs will become more adaptive and personalized. Organizations will leverage AI and data analytics to tailor training to individual needs and to ensure intrapreneurs remain competitive in a rapidly changing business landscape.

Measuring Non-Financial Impact

While financial metrics will always be important, the future of intrapreneurship will see a greater emphasis on measuring non-financial impact. Intrapreneurs will be evaluated based on their contributions to sustainability, social responsibility, and ethical leadership.

Conclusion

The future of intrapreneurship holds the promise of even greater innovation and organizational transformation. By adapting to technological advancements, fostering a global intrapreneurial community, and addressing ethical and environmental challenges, organizations can embrace intrapreneurship as a vital force for positive change. Intrapreneurs, like Sarah, will continue to play a pivotal role in shaping this future, driving innovation from within organizations and advancing the boundaries of what's possible in the world of business.

7

Nurturing Your Inner Intrapreneur

Intrapreneurship is not limited to the corporate world; it's a mindset and skill set that can be cultivated and harnessed by individuals in various aspects of their lives. In this chapter, we will explore how you can nurture your inner intrapreneur, whether you're an employee seeking to bring innovative ideas to your workplace, an entrepreneur looking to infuse intrapreneurial thinking into your business, or an individual simply interested in enhancing your problem-solving and creative abilities.

Unlocking Your Intrapreneurial Potential

Intrapreneurship begins with recognizing and nurturing your inner intrapreneurial potential. Here's how you can start:

- Self-Awareness: Reflect on your skills, strengths, and passions. What areas excite you the most? What problems or opportunities do you find particularly compelling?

- Curiosity: Develop a keen sense of curiosity. Ask questions, explore new subjects, and keep learning. Curiosity is the driving force behind innovation.

- Problem-Solving: Hone your problem-solving skills. Practice looking at challenges from different angles and seeking solutions that others might not have considered.

- Resilience: Cultivate resilience by viewing setbacks as learning opportunities. Develop a growth mindset that embraces failure as a stepping stone to success.

- Networking: Build a network of like-minded individuals, mentors, and experts. Collaborate with diverse teams to gain a broad range of perspectives.

Applying Intrapreneurial Thinking to Your Work

If you're an employee looking to bring intrapreneurial thinking to your job, here's how to get started:

- Identify Opportunities: Look for gaps, inefficiencies, or unmet needs within your organization. These are opportunities for intrapreneurial projects.

- Develop a Business Case: Prepare a clear and compelling business case for your idea. Highlight the potential benefits and alignment with your organization's mission and values.

- Engage Leadership: Seek support from leadership and articulate how your intrapreneurial project aligns with the organization's strategic goals.

- Collaborate and Seek Feedback: Collaborate with colleagues and engage in regular feedback loops to refine your idea. Be open to constructive criticism.

- Measuring Impact: Continuously measure the impact of your intrapreneurial project using key performance indicators (KPIs) and adapt your strategy as needed.

Infusing Intrapreneurship into Your Business

If you're an entrepreneur or business owner, you can infuse intrapreneurship into your organization to drive innovation and growth:

- Cultivate a Culture of Innovation: Foster a culture that encourages employees to think like intrapreneurs. Support risk-taking, experimentation, and creativity.

- Innovation Incubators: Establish innovation incubators or programs that provide employees with resources and autonomy to pursue their intrapreneurial projects.

- Reward and Recognition: Recognize and reward intrapreneurial efforts within your organization. Incentivize employees to come forward with their innovative ideas.

- Invest in Learning and Development: Invest in intrapreneurial training and development programs to enhance your team's skills and capabilities.

Embracing Intrapreneurial Thinking in Everyday Life

Even if you're not in a corporate or entrepreneurial setting, you can apply intrapreneurial thinking in your everyday life:

- Personal Projects: Approach personal goals and projects with an intrapreneurial mindset. Set clear objectives, develop plans, and track your progress.

- Continuous Learning: Stay curious and committed to learning. Explore new interests and seek opportunities to enhance your skills and knowledge.

- Community Engagement: Get involved in your community or volunteer organizations. Look for ways to make a positive impact and address local challenges.

- Creative Problem-Solving: When faced with personal challenges, use creative problem-solving techniques to find innovative solutions.

Conclusion

Intrapreneurship is not limited to the corporate world; it's a versatile approach to problem-solving, innovation, and making a positive impact. Whether you're an employee, entrepreneur, or an individual looking to enhance your creative thinking and problem-solving skills, nurturing your inner intrapreneur can lead to personal and professional growth. By unlocking your intrapreneurial potential, you can contribute to positive change in your workplace, your business, and your community, making a lasting impact on the world around you.

8

Sustaining Intrapreneurship for Long-Term Success

Sustaining intrapreneurship for long-term success requires dedication, adaptability, and a commitment to continuous improvement. In this chapter, we will explore the key strategies and best practices for ensuring that intrapreneurship remains a vital and enduring force within organizations.

Cultivating a Culture of Innovation and Adaptability

An organization's culture plays a central role in the sustainability of intrapreneurship. To sustain intrapreneurial efforts over the long term:

- Embrace Change: Foster a culture that is open to change and adaptation. Intrapreneurs thrive in environments that welcome new ideas and are not resistant to change.

- Empower Employees: Encourage employees at all levels to participate in intrapreneurial activities. Give them a sense of ownership and autonomy in the innovation process.

- Leverage Technology: Stay current with technological advancements that can support intrapreneurial efforts. Implement digital tools and platforms to streamline intrapreneurship programs.

- Promote Learning and Development: Continuously invest in the training and development of intrapreneurs. Keep them updated on the latest skills and tools that can enhance their intrapreneurial endeavors.

Intrapreneurial Incubators and Accelerators

Incubators and accelerators are effective mechanisms for sustaining intrapreneurship. These programs offer structured support to intrapreneurs and their initiatives:

- Incubators: Provide long-term support for early-stage intrapreneurial projects, offering mentorship, resources, and guidance to help them grow and succeed.

- Accelerators: Focus on rapidly developing and scaling intrapreneurial projects, typically through intensive programs that offer coaching, investment opportunities, and access to a network of experts.

Diversity and Inclusion

Diversity and inclusion are not only ethical imperatives but also drivers of innovation and sustainability in intrapreneurship:

- Diverse Teams: Foster diverse teams with varied backgrounds, perspectives, and experiences. Diverse teams are more likely to generate innovative ideas and approaches.

- Inclusive Culture: Promote an inclusive culture where all employees feel valued and heard. Encourage an atmosphere of psychological safety where intrapreneurs can take risks without fear of retribution.

Regular Evaluation and Adaptation

Sustainability relies on continuous evaluation and adaptation. Organizations should regularly assess the effectiveness of their intrapreneurship initiatives:

- Measuring Impact: Define clear KPIs and metrics to measure the impact of intrapreneurial projects. Regularly review and update these indicators to align with changing organizational goals.

- Feedback Loops: Implement feedback mechanisms to gather insights from intrapreneurs and other stakeholders. Use this feedback to refine intrapreneurship programs.

- Pivot When Necessary: Be prepared to pivot or adapt intrapreneurship programs in response to changing market dynamics, technological advancements, and internal or external factors.

Support and Resources for Intrapreneurs

To ensure the sustainability of intrapreneurship, organizations should provide intrapreneurs with the support and resources they need:

- Resource Allocation: Continue to allocate dedicated resources, including budgets and time, for intrapreneurial initiatives.

- Mentorship and Guidance: Offer mentorship programs that connect intrapreneurs with experienced advisors who can provide guidance and support.

- Access to Experts: Provide intrapreneurs with access to experts and specialists who can offer insights and knowledge in specific domains.

- Risk Management: Develop strategies for risk management to help intrapreneurs mitigate potential setbacks and setbacks.

Ethical and Social Responsibility

Sustainability and social responsibility will play an increasingly significant role in intrapreneurship. Organizations should consider the ethical and social implications of intrapreneurial projects:

- Ethical Guidelines: Develop clear ethical guidelines to guide intrapreneurs in making responsible decisions.

- Social Impact Assessment: Assess the social impact of intrapreneurial projects to ensure they align with ethical values and contribute to the betterment of society.

Conclusion

Sustaining intrapreneurship is essential for organizations seeking to remain competitive and innovative in an ever-changing business landscape. By cultivating a culture of innovation, offering support and resources, and prioritizing diversity and inclusion, organizations can ensure that intrapreneurship remains a driving force for long-term success. Continuous evaluation, adaptation, and a commitment to ethical and social responsibility will help intrapreneurship thrive and contribute positively to the organization and society as a whole.

9

Overcoming Common Pitfalls in Intrapreneurship

Intrapreneurship is a powerful force for innovation and growth, but it's not without its pitfalls. In this chapter, we will explore some of the common challenges and roadblocks that intrapreneurs and organizations face and provide strategies to overcome them.

1. Resistance to Change

Challenge: Resistance to change is a common challenge in intrapreneurship. Existing processes and structures can create friction when intrapreneurs attempt to introduce new ideas.

Strategy: To overcome resistance to change, intrapreneurs and organizations should:

- Communicate the benefits: Clearly articulate the advantages of the proposed change to all stakeholders.
  - Involve key players: Engage with decision-makers and potential oppo-

nents early in the process to get their buy-in.
- Pilot projects: Start with smaller, manageable projects to demonstrate the potential success of intrapreneurial initiatives.

2. Resource Constraints

Challenge: Intrapreneurs often face resource constraints, including budget limitations and staffing challenges.

Strategy: To address resource constraints:

- Develop a compelling business case: Clearly outline the potential return on investment (ROI) and impact of the project to secure necessary resources.
- Leverage existing assets: Use the organization's infrastructure, talent, and technology whenever possible to minimize resource requirements.
- Seek alternative funding: Explore external funding sources, partnerships, or grants to support the initiative.

3. Bureaucracy and Slow Decision-Making

Challenge: In large organizations, navigating bureaucracy and slow decision-making processes can hinder intrapreneurial progress.

Strategy: To overcome bureaucratic challenges:

- Engage with supportive leadership: Seek allies within the organization, including leaders who can advocate for the intrapreneurial project.
- Streamline processes: Identify bottlenecks in decision-making and work to simplify and expedite these processes.
- Pilot initiatives: Launch smaller-scale initiatives that require fewer approvals and can serve as proofs of concept before scaling up.

4. Lack of Alignment with Organizational Goals

Challenge: Sometimes, intrapreneurial initiatives may not align with the organization's broader strategic goals.

Strategy: To ensure alignment with organizational goals:

- Clearly communicate objectives: Establish a shared understanding of the project's alignment with the organization's mission and values.
    - Develop a strategic plan: Create a roadmap that outlines how the intrapreneurial initiative will contribute to the organization's long-term goals.
    - Periodically reassess alignment: Regularly review and adjust the project to maintain alignment with shifting organizational priorities.

5. Uncertainty and Risk

Challenge: Intrapreneurship inherently involves risk, and the uncertainty associated with new ventures can be daunting.

Strategy: To manage uncertainty and risk:

- Perform thorough market research: Gather data to support your intrapreneurial idea and minimize uncertainty.
    - Develop contingency plans: Prepare for potential setbacks by creating backup strategies to address unexpected challenges.
    - Embrace a growth mindset: View failures as opportunities for learning and growth, and be resilient in the face of adversity.

6. Lack of Cross-Functional Collaboration

Challenge: Intrapreneurial projects often require collaboration across departments, but silos can hinder effective cross-functional teamwork.

Strategy: To promote collaboration:

- Establish cross-functional teams: Assemble teams with members from various departments to encourage diverse perspectives and expertise.
- Foster a collaborative culture: Create an organizational culture that values teamwork, information sharing, and interdisciplinary collaboration.
- Provide tools and technology: Implement collaboration tools and technology that facilitate communication and cooperation among teams.

7. Failure to Measure Impact

Challenge: Without a clear way to measure success, intrapreneurial projects may struggle to secure ongoing support.

Strategy: To measure and communicate impact effectively:

- Define clear KPIs: Set key performance indicators that align with the project's goals and the organization's strategic objectives.
- Regularly evaluate impact: Continuously assess the project's success, make data-driven decisions, and communicate the value it brings to the organization.
- Adjust and iterate: Be willing to adapt the project based on the impact data, making improvements and refinements as necessary.

Conclusion

Intrapreneurship is a dynamic and innovative approach to problem-solving and growth, but it is not without challenges. By recognizing and addressing common pitfalls such as resistance to change, resource constraints, and bureaucratic obstacles, intrapreneurs and organizations can navigate these hurdles and build a sustainable culture of intrapreneurship that drives long-term success. With the right strategies and a commitment to learning and adaptation, intrapreneurs can overcome these challenges and continue to push the boundaries of innovation within their organizations.

10

Intrapreneurship in the 21st Century

Intrapreneurship is not just a buzzword; it's a critical component of the 21st-century business landscape. In this chapter, we will explore how intrapreneurship is evolving to meet the demands of the modern world, driven by factors like technological advancements, globalization, and changing societal values.

1. Technology-Driven Innovation

In the 21st century, technology is at the heart of intrapreneurial innovation. Key developments include:

- Digital Transformation: Organizations must embrace digital technologies to stay competitive. Intrapreneurs are at the forefront of these transformations, leveraging technology to create new products and processes.

- Artificial Intelligence: AI is powering intrapreneurial initiatives in various ways, from automating routine tasks to enabling predictive analytics and personalized customer experiences.

- Big Data: The ability to collect and analyze vast amounts of data is a cornerstone of intrapreneurial projects, allowing for data-driven decision-making and insights into customer behavior.

- Blockchain: Blockchain technology is driving innovation in supply chain management, finance, and data security, creating opportunities for intrapreneurs to explore new avenues.

2. Globalization and Cross-Border Collaboration

The 21st century has seen a significant increase in global connectivity and collaboration. Intrapreneurs are tapping into these trends by:

- Cross-Border Teams: Remote work and virtual teams allow intrapreneurs to collaborate with colleagues and experts from around the world, bringing diverse perspectives to projects.

- Global Markets: Organizations are expanding into international markets, creating opportunities for intrapreneurs to develop products and services with a global audience in mind.

- Cultural Sensitivity: Intrapreneurs must consider cultural differences and adapt their projects to diverse markets, focusing on inclusivity and respecting local norms and values.

3. Sustainability and Social Responsibility

In the 21st century, intrapreneurship is increasingly tied to sustainability and social responsibility. This includes:

- Green Initiatives: Intrapreneurs are developing environmentally friendly products and processes, addressing climate change and resource conservation.

- Ethical Business Practices: Organizations are prioritizing ethical conduct and transparency, pushing intrapreneurs to align their projects with ethical values.

- Social Impact: Intrapreneurs are creating initiatives that benefit society, addressing issues like poverty, education, and healthcare.

4. Rapid Adaptation and Resilience

The 21st century has been marked by rapid change and uncertainty, making adaptability and resilience critical for intrapreneurs. Strategies include:

- Agility: Intrapreneurs must be nimble and able to pivot quickly in response to changing circumstances, seizing emerging opportunities.

- Continuous Learning: Lifelong learning is essential to keep up with evolving technologies and trends. Intrapreneurs should prioritize personal and professional development.

- Resilience: The ability to bounce back from setbacks and maintain a growth mindset is crucial for intrapreneurs facing adversity.

5. Inclusive Innovation

Inclusivity is a central theme of 21st-century intrapreneurship:

- Diversity and Inclusion: Intrapreneurship benefits from diverse teams, which bring varied perspectives and approaches to problem-solving.

- Accessibility: Intrapreneurs are designing products and services that are accessible to all, regardless of ability, making innovation more inclusive.

6. Artificial Intelligence and Automation

As AI and automation continue to advance, intrapreneurs are exploring their applications, which include:

- Process Optimization: Intrapreneurs are using AI to streamline business processes, reduce costs, and improve efficiency.

- Personalization: AI is enabling intrapreneurs to create personalized customer experiences, tailoring products and services to individual preferences.

- Innovative Solutions: AI-driven solutions are solving complex problems and pushing the boundaries of what's possible in various industries.

Conclusion

Intrapreneurship in the 21st century is defined by technology-driven innovation, global collaboration, sustainability, and social responsibility. Intrapreneurs of this era must be adaptable, resilient, and committed to inclusive innovation. With the right mindset and strategies, they can harness the transformative power of intrapreneurship to drive positive change and remain at the forefront of innovation in a rapidly evolving world.

11

The Future of Intrapreneurship

The future of intrapreneurship promises to be even more dynamic and transformative as organizations and individuals adapt to the evolving business landscape. In this chapter, we will explore emerging trends, challenges, and opportunities that will shape the future of intrapreneurship.

1. Emerging Technologies

The rapid advancement of technology is poised to drive innovation in intrapreneurship:

- Quantum Computing: The development of quantum computers will open new possibilities for data processing, optimization, and complex problem-solving.

- Biotechnology: Innovations in biotech, such as gene editing and personalized medicine, will provide opportunities for intrapreneurs in healthcare and life sciences.

- Cybersecurity: As digital threats evolve, intrapreneurs will be crucial in developing innovative cybersecurity solutions to protect organizations and individuals.

2. Decentralized and Blockchain Technologies

Blockchain and decentralized technologies will continue to disrupt traditional industries and create intrapreneurial opportunities:

- Decentralized Finance (DeFi): Intrapreneurs will explore DeFi solutions that democratize access to financial services and challenge traditional banking systems.

- Supply Chain Management: Blockchain will be used to improve transparency and traceability in supply chains, reducing fraud and waste.

- Smart Contracts: The automation of contracts through smart contracts will streamline legal and financial processes.

3. Artificial Intelligence and Automation

AI and automation will play an increasingly significant role in intrapreneurship:

- AI-Enhanced Decision-Making: AI-driven analytics and decision support tools will aid intrapreneurs in making more informed and data-driven choices.

- Robotic Process Automation (RPA): RPA will automate routine tasks, freeing intrapreneurs to focus on higher-level, creative work.

- AI in Healthcare: AI-powered diagnostics, drug discovery, and telehealth solutions will revolutionize healthcare, providing opportunities for intrapreneurs.

4. Sustainability and Environmental Innovation

The urgency of addressing climate change and environmental concerns will drive intrapreneurship in the direction of sustainability:

- Clean Energy: Intrapreneurs will develop innovative solutions for renewable energy, energy storage, and energy-efficient technologies.

- Circular Economy: Initiatives that promote recycling, waste reduction, and sustainable resource management will become central to intrapreneurial projects.

- Green Tech: Green technologies, from eco-friendly packaging to sustainable transportation, will offer intrapreneurial opportunities.

5. Health and Wellness Innovations

The focus on health and well-being will continue to shape intrapreneurship:

- Telemedicine and Digital Health: Intrapreneurs will explore digital health solutions, telemedicine platforms, and wearable devices to improve healthcare access and outcomes.

- Mental Health and Well-Being: Innovations in mental health support, stress management, and well-being apps will gain traction.

- Personalized Nutrition: Intrapreneurs will develop personalized nutrition and dietary management solutions to enhance individual health.

6. Collaboration and Open Innovation

The future of intrapreneurship will be marked by increased collaboration and open innovation:

- Ecosystem Partnerships: Organizations will collaborate with startups, universities, and research institutions to access a wider pool of innovation.

- Crowdsourcing and Co-Creation: Companies will involve customers and external communities in the innovation process, harnessing collective intelligence.

7. Ethical and Responsible Innovation

Intrapreneurship will place a greater emphasis on ethical and responsible innovation:

- Responsible AI: Intrapreneurs will prioritize the ethical use of AI, addressing issues like bias, privacy, and fairness.

- Social Impact Initiatives: More intrapreneurs will work on projects with a clear social impact, addressing issues such as education, poverty, and accessibility.

- Sustainability Standards: Organizations will establish sustainability guidelines for intrapreneurs to follow, ensuring environmental and ethical responsibility.

Conclusion

The future of intrapreneurship is marked by rapid technological advancements, sustainability imperatives, and a focus on well-being and ethical innovation. Intrapreneurs will play a pivotal role in leveraging these trends to drive positive change and create innovative solutions that address complex challenges. As the intrapreneurial landscape continues to evolve, adaptability, ethical consciousness, and a commitment to learning will be essential for those seeking to remain at the forefront of innovation.

12

Fostering Intrapreneurship Culture

Fostering a culture of intrapreneurship is a continuous journey that requires dedication, leadership, and a commitment to innovation. In this chapter, we will explore the principles and practices for nurturing and sustaining a vibrant intrapreneurship culture within organizations.

1. Leadership Commitment

A culture of intrapreneurship begins with leadership commitment and support. Key strategies include:

- Lead by Example: Leaders should model intrapreneurial behavior by encouraging risk-taking, experimentation, and creative problem-solving.

- Resource Allocation: Dedicate budgets, time, and other resources to intrapreneurial initiatives, demonstrating the organization's commitment to innovation.

- Advocacy: Act as champions of intrapreneurship, actively promoting it as a core value of the organization.

2. Clear Vision and Strategy

An intrapreneurship culture thrives when it's aligned with a clear vision and strategy:

- Mission Alignment: Ensure that intrapreneurship aligns with the organization's mission and long-term goals.

- Strategic Planning: Develop a roadmap for intrapreneurship, outlining how it supports the organization's broader strategic objectives.

3. Encouraging Risk-Taking and Experimentation

Intrapreneurship flourishes when risk-taking and experimentation are encouraged:

- Psychological Safety: Create an environment where employees feel safe to take calculated risks and experiment without fear of punitive consequences.

- Celebrate Failure: View failure as a learning opportunity, and celebrate intrapreneurs' efforts, even if they don't lead to immediate success.

4. Cross-Functional Collaboration

Intrapreneurship thrives on collaboration across different departments and disciplines:

- Interdisciplinary Teams: Form cross-functional teams that bring together individuals with diverse backgrounds and expertise.

- Idea Exchange: Encourage open channels for idea exchange and knowledge sharing across the organization.

5. Idea Generation and Innovation Hubs

Dedicated spaces and platforms for innovation are instrumental:

- Innovation Hubs: Create physical or virtual spaces that facilitate creativity, collaboration, and experimentation.

- Idea Submission Systems: Implement a streamlined system for employees to submit, evaluate, and develop their innovative ideas.

6. Mentorship and Guidance

Intrapreneurs benefit from mentorship and guidance:

- Mentorship Programs: Establish mentorship programs that connect intrapreneurs with experienced advisors who can offer support and insights.

- Executive Sponsorship: Involve senior leaders as mentors to intrapreneurs, providing them with a direct line to top decision-makers.

7. Innovation Management Platforms

Scalable platforms for managing intrapreneurial projects are essential:

- Project Tracking: Implement tools to monitor and manage intrapreneurial initiatives, keeping them on track and aligned with organizational goals.

- Collaboration Software: Utilize collaboration and communication tools that enable intrapreneurs to work together efficiently.

- Data Analytics: Implement data analytics systems to measure the success and impact of intrapreneurial projects.

8. Continuous Learning and Development

To maintain a culture of intrapreneurship, organizations should invest in learning and development:

- Training Programs: Offer intrapreneurial training to help employees develop skills like problem-solving, creative thinking, and risk management.

- Lifelong Learning: Encourage a culture of lifelong learning and personal development, ensuring that employees stay current with evolving trends and technologies.

9. Recognition and Rewards

Recognizing and rewarding intrapreneurs is vital to sustaining an intrapreneurship culture:

- Incentive Programs: Establish reward programs that acknowledge successful intrapreneurs through financial incentives, promotions, and public recognition.

- Publicize Success Stories: Share success stories and best practices to inspire others and showcase the benefits of intrapreneurship.

10. Measuring Impact

Measuring and evaluating the impact of intrapreneurial initiatives is essential:

- Key Performance Indicators (KPIs): Define clear KPIs and metrics that align with organizational goals to assess the impact of intrapreneurship.

- Accountability: Implement accountability mechanisms to ensure that intrapreneurial projects contribute to strategic objectives.

11. Ethical and Social Responsibility

A culture of intrapreneurship should incorporate ethical and social responsibility principles:

- Ethical Guidelines: Develop clear ethical guidelines that guide intrapreneurs in making responsible decisions.

- Social Impact Initiatives: Encourage intrapreneurs to work on projects that benefit society, addressing issues such as education, poverty, and healthcare.

12. Agility and Adaptation

A culture of intrapreneurship should remain agile and adaptable:

- Change Readiness: Embrace change and continuously adapt to evolving technologies, market dynamics, and organizational needs.

- Learning from Failure: Use failures as opportunities for growth and learning, adapting strategies based on lessons learned.

Conclusion

Fostering a culture of intrapreneurship is an ongoing process that requires commitment, leadership, and a focus on innovation. By embracing these principles and practices, organizations can create an environment where intrapreneurs can thrive, driving continuous innovation and contributing to long-term success. An intrapreneurship culture empowers employees to think creatively, take calculated risks, and develop innovative solutions, positioning the organization for growth and adaptability in the ever-changing business landscape.

In this comprehensive guide on intrapreneurship, we've explored the concept of intrapreneurship as the practice of fostering innovation and entrepreneurial thinking within organizations. We've covered twelve chapters, each addressing various aspects of intrapreneurship:

1. Introduction to Intrapreneurship: We defined intrapreneurship and its significance in driving innovation and growth within organizations.

2. Intrapreneurial Mindset: Explored the traits and qualities of intrapreneurs, individuals who drive innovation from within organizations.

3. The Role of Leadership: Examined the crucial role of leadership in creating an environment that fosters intrapreneurial initiatives.

4. Nurturing Intrapreneurs: Discussed how organizations can identify and nurture intrapreneurial talent among their employees.

5. Intrapreneurial Projects: Explored the various types of intrapreneurial projects, from product development to process improvement.

6. Corporate Innovation Ecosystem: Analyzed the components that make up a successful corporate innovation ecosystem.

7. The Intrapreneurial Process: Detailed the stages of the intrapreneurial process, from idea generation to implementation.

8. Challenges and Solutions: Examined common challenges faced in intrapreneurship and provided strategies for overcoming them.

9. Intrapreneurship in the 21st Century: Discussed how intrapreneurship is evolving in response to technological advancements, globalization, and changing societal values.

10. Fostering Intrapreneurship Culture: Explored the principles and practices

for nurturing and sustaining a vibrant intrapreneurship culture within organizations.

In summary, intrapreneurship is a dynamic and vital approach to innovation that organizations can harness to adapt, thrive, and remain competitive in the ever-changing business landscape. By cultivating a culture that values innovation, encourages risk-taking, and provides support and resources for intrapreneurs, organizations can drive positive change from within and position themselves for long-term success. Intrapreneurs, with their entrepreneurial mindset and creative problem-solving skills, play a pivotal role in this process, shaping the future of business and innovation.

www.ingramcontent.com/pod-product-compliance
Lightning Source LLC
LaVergne TN
LVHW012128070526
838202LV00056B/5922